Three features of this del
and impressive. First, Rag
exposition and defense of the importance of truth
and what one believes for the Christian life. Sadly,
this factor is often left out of such books, and it is
refreshing to see it front and center. Second, Ragsdale
makes a very, very important set of distinctions among
essential, important, and personal elements of one's
overall belief system. And he follows this with deep and
crucial reflection about how to treat non-essentials and
those with whom we disagree. These factors alone are
worth reading the book. I highly recommend *Christian
Convictions*. It fills a vacuum in the literature.

— J. P. Moreland, PhD, Distinguished Professor of
Philosophy, Talbot School of Theology; author of
Finding Quiet

Few authors have the gift to weave sound theology with
practical advice like Dr. Chad Ragsdale. His new book
Christian Convictions is a must-read that will help you
to know what you believe and how to engage graciously
those who disagree with you. With a shepherd's heart, a
scholar's mind, and a friend's words, Dr. Chad Ragsdale
guides us to effectively engage society in love and truth.

— Caleb Kaltenbach, author of *God of Tomorrow*
and *Messy Grace*; founder of
The Messy Grace Group

I've always loved the slogan, "In essentials, unity; in nonessentials, liberty; and in all things, love." Sometimes, however, our slogans hang on the church wall but don't happen down the church hall. How can we move this wisdom from poster to practice? Chad Ragsdale answers that question, writing in the same spirit Alexander Campbell and Paul himself wrote. You'll want to buy this biblical, practical, readable booklet in bulk for your leaders (or your whole congregation).

— Matt Proctor, President,
Ozark Christian College

CHAD RAGSDALE

THE REAL LIFE THEOLOGY SERIES

CHRISTIAN CONVICTIONS

DISCERNING THE ESSENTIAL, IMPORTANT, AND PERSONAL ELEMENTS

3

R E N Ǝ W.org

Christian Convictions: Discerning the Essential, Important, and Personal Elements

ISBN (paperback) 978-1-949921-51-9
ISBN (Mobi) 978-1-949921-52-6
ISBN (ePub) 978-1-949921-53-3

Cover and interior design by Harrington Interactive Media (harringtoninteractive.com)

Printed in the United States of America

To my mom and dad,
who were my first teachers of models
of the essentials of Christian belief

CONTENTS

GENERAL EDITORS' NOTE

The Bible teaches us many truths. How do we understand the importance of these teachings? Are they all equally important? Some seem to be more important than others. In fact, some teachings appear to be core to the faith, while others seem to be comparatively peripheral.

Chad Ragsdale is uniquely qualified to help us sort out elements of the faith that are essential, important, and personal. Chad is the Academic Dean at Ozark Christian College, where he has served on the faculty since 2005. He teaches primarily in the areas of Christian apologetics, philosophy, and biblical interpretation. Chad has been married to his wife, Tara, since 2001 and has three kids, Logan, Adeline, and Ryane. He has a Bachelor of Arts in Preaching and a Master of Divinity in Contemporary Theology—both from Lincoln Christian University. He has a Doctor of

Ministry in Engaging Mind and Culture from Talbot School of Theology.

This book expounds on the section from the Renew.org Leaders' Faith Statement called "Christian Convictions":

> We believe the Scriptures reveal three distinct elements of the faith: essential elements which are necessary for salvation; important elements which are to be pursued so that we faithfully follow Christ; and personal elements or opinion. The gospel is essential. Every person who is indwelt and sealed by God's Holy Spirit because of their faith in the gospel is a brother or a sister in Christ. Important but secondary elements of the faith are vital. Our faithfulness to God requires us to seek and pursue them, even as we acknowledge that our salvation may not be dependent on getting them right. And third, there are personal matters of opinion, disputable areas where God gives us personal freedom. But we are never at liberty to express our freedom in a way that causes others to stumble in sin. In all things, we want to show understanding, kindness, and love.
>
> *See the full Network Faith Statements at the end of this book.

Support Scriptures: 1 Corinthians 15:1–8;
Romans 1:15–17; Galatians 1:6–9;
2 Timothy 2:8; Ephesians 1:13–14; 4:4–6;
Romans 8:9; 1 Corinthians 12:13;
1 Timothy 4:16; 2 Timothy 3:16–4:4;
Matthew 15:6–9; Acts 20:32; 1 Corinthians 11:1–2;
1 John 2:3–4; 2 Peter 3:14–16; Romans 14:1–23.

The following tips might help you use this book more effectively (and the other books in the *Real Life Theology* series):

1. *Five questions, answers, and Scriptures.* We framed this book around five key questions with five short answers and five notable Scriptures. This format provides clarity, making it easier to commit crucial information to memory. This format also enables the books in the *Real Life Theology* series to support our catechism. Our catechism is a series of fixed questions and answers for instruction in church or home. In all, the series has fifty-two questions, answers, and key Scriptures. This particular book focuses on the five that are most pertinent to Christian convictions.

2. *Personal reflection.* At the end of each chapter are six reflection questions. Each chapter is short and intended for everyday people to read and then

process. The questions help you to engage the specific teachings and, if you prefer, to journal your practical reflections.

3. *Discussion questions.* The reflection questions double as discussion-group questions. Even if you do not write down the answers, the questions can be used to stimulate group conversation.

4. *Summary videos.* You can find three to seven-minute video teachings that summarize the book, as well as each chapter, at Renew.org. These short videos can function as standalone teachings. But for groups or group leaders using the book, they can also be used to launch discussion of the reading.

May God use this book to fuel faithful and effective disciple making in your life and church.

For King Jesus,
Bobby Harrington and Daniel McCoy
General Editors, *Real Life Theology* series

INTRODUCTION

I still remember approaching my dad at the campfire that night. It was the summer of my seventh-grade year, and we were at one of my favorite places on earth: summer camp at Lake Region Christian Assembly. My dad was the dean of the week, and I was a camper with a spiritual dilemma that had been stirring within me all week. I was baptized into Christ very young, at the age of seven. I remember being deeply troubled by how much more I knew about Jesus at the age of thirteen than I did when I was seven. This seems a little funny to say now that I am in my forties looking back at what I thought I knew when I was thirteen. It is now obvious to me that we naturally continue to grow and progress in all sorts of ways as we age, but as a middle school student, my spiritual growth was causing me anxiety. Attending camp that week had the twin effect of both spurring on my faith yet arousing the fear that perhaps my baptism was not sufficient. Had I really known enough at my baptism in order to be saved? So after our evening worship around the campfire, I went to my dad with a simple question: "Do I need to get baptized again?"

In some sense, this book is about my dad's answer to that question. His answer was twofold. First, he reminded me about one of the most important truths of discipleship: we are always in the process of growth. He assured me that if I did not know more about Jesus at thirteen than at seven, then there would be something terribly wrong with my development. He told me that he was still learning new and exciting things every day as he followed Jesus. He was also constantly reminded of his need for Jesus. In those moments, he told me, we need not fret about whether our baptism was enough. Instead, we celebrate the unending truth of our baptism. A line I have used with my own kids is, "God's grace does not need booster shots."

Second, he reminded me that the basic truths of my faith had not changed; I had simply come to understand them at a deeper level. We briefly walked through those essential things that Christians believe. With a father's pastoral care, he assured me that I had "known enough" to be baptized even at a young

> THE BASIC TRUTHS OF MY FAITH HAD NOT CHANGED; I HAD SIMPLY COME TO UNDERSTAND THEM AT A DEEPER LEVEL.

age. The essential beliefs that were "enough" are the focus of this brief book.

Following an earthquake in the ancient city of Philippi, a terrified jailer kneeled before Paul and Silas and asked a pressing question: "What must I do to be saved?" (Acts 16:30b). This is like the question my thirteen-year-old self asked and what many people continue to ask: "What must we believe to be saved?"

People approach this question in different ways. It has become fashionable for many today to wonder if it matters at all what a person believes. This will be the subject of the first chapter of this book. Others are confident that what a person believes matters, but they struggle to distinguish between beliefs that are essential for salvation, beliefs that are important in order to faithfully follow Christ, and beliefs that are personal preferences or opinions. Chapters 2 and 3 are dedicated to identifying these different kinds of Christian beliefs.

The final two chapters are dedicated to addressing practical concerns related to beliefs: How should we treat those elements of our faith that are not essential for salvation? How should we treat those who disagree with us on matters of belief? As in all things, we will take our cues principally from the pages of Scripture. We recognize that answering these questions is complex, but we can do no better than to seek the wisdom and truth found in God's Word. That is my primary aim, but as I answer, I also want to capture my father's pastoral care in the way I answer these questions. Seeking to understand Christian beliefs—and their level of importance—is not merely an intellectual exercise; identifying the truths of our faith cuts to the very core of life and salvation.

1

DOES WHAT WE BELIEVE REALLY MATTER?

Answer: Yes. To have faith is not simply a feeling or emotion. Faith begins with believing that certain things are true about God and his Son, Jesus.

For God so loved the world that he gave his one and only Son, that whoever believes in him shall not perish but have eternal life.
— John 3:16

Starting in the spring of 2020, much of society temporarily shut down because of the COVID-19 pandemic. These shutdowns, of course, dramatically affected local churches because they were forced, in many cases, to stop meeting in person for worship. Laura Kelly, the governor of Kansas, faced criticism for her decision to shut down churches in her state, and defended her stance:

> Religion is really not about the building. It's about the faith, it's about how it feels on the inside. The need to congregate is important but not during a pandemic. . . . I am not trying to suppress religion. I'm just trying to save Kansans' lives.[1]

There is a lot we could say about this statement, but for the purposes of this chapter, I want to focus on the second sentence, "It's about the faith, it's about how it feels on the inside." I agree that faith is more important than buildings, but is it true that faith is about "how it feels on the inside"?

To answer this question, let us turn first to the biblical Gospels. In the Gospel of John, the word "believe" appears ninety-eight times in its twenty-one chapters. In the overwhelming majority of those cases, belief is directed toward a person—Jesus. John 3:16 is the most famous example, but another good example is

John 11:25: "I am the resurrection and the life. The one who believes in me will live, even though they die."[2] What is most important to Jesus is that people would believe in him and be saved. We observe a similar idea in Matthew's Gospel. For example, Jesus asked Peter a critical question: "Who do you say I am?" Peter responded by affirming, "You are the Messiah, the Son of the living God" (Matthew 16:15–16). It is Peter's true confession of Jesus' identity, not simply his feelings, which serves as the bedrock foundation for the church.

BELIEVING WITH THE WHOLE SELF

IN THE LETTERS OF Paul, we discover a consistent emphasis on believing rightly. One of the best and simplest examples is in Romans 10:9–10.

> If you declare with your mouth, "Jesus is Lord," and believe in your heart that God raised him from the dead, you will be saved. For it is with your heart that you believe and are justified, and it is with your mouth that you profess your faith and are saved.

The modern reader might read this and associate "heart" with "feelings," but this would be a mistake. To the ancients, a person's heart did not primarily represent their feelings. It represented the innermost being of a person. To believe with your heart means that you believe something beyond superficial faith. It means that you have believed with your whole self. To Paul here, much like to Jesus in the Gospels, salvation is tied to what the saved believe. The notion that faith is merely about feelings would have been foreign to Paul.

Now, it is important to know that biblical faith in Jesus is not *merely* about belief. The book of James reminds us that "faith by itself, if it is not accompanied by action, is dead" (James 2:17). Paul agrees with this in the Romans passage above! He reminds us in the passage above that believing in Jesus is more than just an intellectual exercise; we believe with our hearts and minds. Our beliefs bring about an effect in every part of us. This idea is also at the core of what Jesus called the Greatest Commandment. He told us to love God "with all your heart and with all your soul and with all your mind" (Matthew 22:37). Our belief really looks a lot like love in a marriage. It is comprehensive; it includes affection, trust, faithfulness, and loyalty.[3] The Greek word for "faith" in the New Testament is *pistis*. It encompasses everything you would find in a loyal relationship between a husband and wife that endures over the decades. So faith is more than belief, but we must add that believing is never *less* than affirming certain truths with our intellect. Loving God is difficult without any knowledge of who that God is. This leads me to my next point.

MANY PATHS UP THE SAME MOUNTAIN?

Despite what Scripture says, it is fashionable for some in our culture to insist that it does not really matter what you believe about God or religion. To these religious relativists, religious beliefs are different from other kinds of beliefs like beliefs about science, mathematics, or even history. The assumption is that specific beliefs about God are like opinions on music: everyone has their own preference and no one is any closer to the truth than the next person. They sometimes compare beliefs about God to taking different paths up a mountain. The paths might be different, but the destination is ultimately the same. So when it comes to God, distinct beliefs do not matter. Religious beliefs are merely about personal preferences and not about what is objectively true.

We should point out that there is a fundamental problem with this many-paths-up-the-same-mountain illustration. It assumes that God is simply a place. If God were a place, then the illustration would work because we can of course take multiple paths to get to the same place. But God is not a place; God is a person.

Remembering how Jesus talks about faith in the Gospel of John, we know that God calls us not to believe in abstractions but in him as a person (John 11:25). He calls us to believe *in him*. This sort of faith in Jesus is personal and exclusive. This kind of faith might be illustrated by a marriage relationship. What does it mean for me to "believe in" my wife? Well, my belief in this case would look a lot like trust, commitment, and even love. My belief in my wife is personal and exclusive to her. I

GOD CALLS US NOT TO BELIEVE IN ABSTRACTIONS BUT IN HIM AS A PERSON.

do not believe in my wife and love her well by committing myself to other women. Such a belief would be adulterous. It is not by accident that the false worship of idolatry in the Bible is so often compared to adultery (e.g., Ezekiel 23:37; Jeremiah 3:8–9; Hosea 1:2). Believing in other gods creates a fracture in our relationship with the living God.

There are consequences to assuming that beliefs do not really matter. For example, according to Barna, almost half of practicing Christian millennials say it is wrong to try to evangelize people of other religions.[4] This statistic reveals how many who self-identify as Christians today do not think specific beliefs matter. Why else would they think it's wrong to evangelize? This shows that when people reduce religion to feelings and faith to opinions, the passion for spreading the life-saving truth of the gospel wanes. Tragically, we often find that a faith emptied of concrete beliefs soon becomes no faith at all. On the other hand, we know that believing in Jesus and following him is the only path to freedom (see John 8:31–32). The truth of Jesus sets us free from the power of sin and from the lies that masquerade as truth in this world. What we believe about God matters. It matters for true life and for salvation.

1. It has become a common assumption that religious faith is about personal preference and feelings rather than truth. Therefore, no one is either right or wrong when it comes to issues of faith. One of the many problems with this assumption is that it seems to ignore the fact that our feelings often steer us in wrong or even dangerous directions. When have your feelings led you down a dangerous road?

_____

_____

_____

_____

_____

_____

2. Hebrews 11 is sometimes called "the faith chapter" because of its detailed description of faith drawing upon examples from the Old Testament. This chapter is punctuated in Hebrews 12:1–3 by the ultimate example of faith found in Jesus. Take a few minutes and read Hebrews 11:1–12:3. How would you define biblical faith as described in this passage?

_____

_____

_____

3. What changes would you need to make in your relationship with God to be able to call your faith "personal and exclusive"?

_____

_____

_____

4. Why do some Christians feel hesitant to share the gospel with others? Why do some even see evangelism as wrong?

_____

_____

_____

5. In John 8:31–36, Jesus connects the knowledge of truth with freedom. How does Jesus define truth and freedom in this passage? How would you respond if somebody asked you what truth is? What freedom is?

_____

_____

_____

_____

_____

_____

6. What actions will you take to pursue a rock-solid faith based on biblical truths that goes beyond the highs and the lows of your feelings?

_____

_____

_____

_____

_____

_____

2

WHAT IS THE DIFFERENCE BETWEEN ESSENTIAL, IMPORTANT, AND PERSONAL ELEMENTS?

Answer: Essential elements are necessary for salvation. Important elements do not save us, but are necessary in order to follow Jesus faithfully. Personal elements are based on marginal convictions or preferences.

There is one body and one Spirit, just as you were called to one hope when you were called; one Lord, one faith, one baptism; one God and Father of all, who is over all and through all and in all.
— Ephesians 4:4–6

n the last chapter, we established that our beliefs about God matter, but not every belief matters in the same way. For instance, I believe that Mercury is the planet that orbits closest to the sun, but while that belief is true, it does not necessarily *matter* for how we live our lives. We have many beliefs just like that—beliefs that are true yet inconsequential. Likewise, we have other beliefs that may be proven incorrect at some point in time to relatively little consequence. If I believe that the Chicago Cubs will likely win today, for example, but they end up losing, my life will not have changed other than some mild frustration. In addition, we each have a host of personal preferences and personal opinions that may be true for us but not for others. Many of these preferences are also relatively inconsequential for others, even though they may be meaningful for me. My preference for Mexican food over Italian food does not mean that Mexican food is better than Italian food for everyone, just me and others with that preference.

We also have beliefs we hold that are very consequential. I am not a good swimmer, for example, which has been confirmed by multiple negative experiences I've had trying to swim. If I were to believe that I am a good swimmer, that could actually put my life at risk. My beliefs about my swimming abilities matter

SOME BELIEFS ARE ESSENTIAL FOR LIFE AND WELL-BEING.

differently than my preference for Mexican food. As another example of how beliefs can matter or not, my belief in the orbital position of Mercury does not matter, but my belief in the connection between smoking and cancer does. The point here is that when it comes to beliefs and how we live them out, they do not all matter in the same way. Some beliefs are essential for life and well-being. Some are not essential, but they are still very important. Other beliefs matter only as far as our personal preferences matter to us. Many of our beliefs fall somewhere on this spectrum of categories.

SPECTRUM OF THEOLOGICAL BELIEFS

OUR BELIEFS ABOUT GOD are similar: not all of our beliefs matter in the same way. There are some beliefs that we can call "essential for salvation." These beliefs are so important that not believing them keeps a person from being saved. Other beliefs we can call "essential for orthodoxy." Orthodoxy, in this case, simply means "proper belief." We ought to pursue these so that we can faithfully follow Christ. They are important enough that if we get them wrong, we will need correction and instruction. Our salvation, however, is not determined by our ability to get all of these beliefs exactly right. Finally, there are many beliefs, especially those about the practice of faith, that qualify as personal preferences in our relationship with God. They may be very important to an individual or to a group of like-minded people, but they are not essential for salvation or important for living a faithful life. These three categories are the essential, important, and personal elements of our faith.

In discussing these essential, important, and personal elements, we are not just talking about the truths we believe but also how we respond to these truths by faith. Faith is the language of our relationship with God; faith is a living, breathing thing. By faith we seek God, repent from sin, obey the teachings of Jesus, and live in step with the Spirit (Hebrews 11:6; Galatians 5:16–21). Faith is the essential human response to God and his grace (Ephesians 2:8–9).

It can be a challenge for us to properly distinguish between essential, important, and personal elements. What one person labels as merely "important," another person might call "essential." Another person might take a belief that should rightly be called essential and relegate it to the realm of personal preferences. I dedicate the next chapter to identifying what Scripture calls essential, but in this chapter, I describe two exercises I've used with college-age students that have helped them identify essential beliefs. May these exercises help you to begin thinking in these categories.

EXERCISE 1: WRITING A PARAGRAPH

FIRST, GET OUT A blank sheet of paper and write a short paragraph summarizing what you consider to be your most important beliefs about God. When I issue this exercise in class, I give my students only one minute to write a maximum of three sentences, and then they read them aloud or turn them in to me. It sounds daunting at first. How can a person—especially a Bible college student eager to impress their professor—possibly summarize their beliefs about God with such limitations? With libraries literally full of books reflecting on the depths of theology, it seems almost wrong even to have students attempt to summarize essential beliefs in this way. The benefit of the exercise, however, is that it functions sort of like a fire drill in the mind. If you had to exit the house quickly and could only take what you could carry, what would you take? The pressure surfaces what really matters to a person versus what is merely important.

After I have them write their paragraphs, I usually have a few students volunteer to read what they have written. This sparks a fun conversation and analysis among the students about what beliefs really matter. Using this exercise, I have gotten some extremely thoughtful and impressive paragraphs through the years. I encourage my students to do two things with their paragraphs: First, I encourage them to critically examine what they have written. Without giving them any time constraints, I have them go back to their paragraph in private and carefully ask themselves why they wrote what they did. *Would you change anything? If so, why?* Second, I encourage the students to repeat the exercise from time to time in order to continue clarifying their thinking.

EXERCISE 2: DRAWING A BULLSEYE

THE SECOND EXERCISE THAT I use to help students identify their core beliefs involves drawing a large target with three concentric circles on the board. The target represents all of their beliefs about God. I ask them, "What is at the bullseye of your target?" The bullseye is necessarily small, so not much can or should fit in the bullseye. "Bullseye beliefs" are our immovable and foundational beliefs about God that are so important that, if they were to change, everything else in our lives would have to change as a result. "Important beliefs" may come close to the bullseye of the target and still others are on the outer edges of the target.

I usually illustrate the usefulness of the target exercise with several examples. One of my favorite examples is dinosaurs. Teaching apologetics for many years, I have come to dislike some questions. I dislike them not because they are inappropriate, but because they miss what is essential and even what is important. "What does the Bible say about dinosaurs?" is one of those questions. I just do not really care because even if we were to find them in the Bible, it does not matter. I think dinosaurs are cool, mind you, but finding them in the Bible is not anywhere near the center of my target. My faith does not rise or fall based on what the Bible says about the Tyrannosaurus Rex.

Another example I use to show the importance of the target exercise is the story of Jonah: "Is the story of Jonah real history or is it meant as a sort of allegory?" I ask. There are different perspectives on this, even among Old Testament scholars. Without providing an answer to the question, I ask the class where the importance of answering such a question should be placed on the target. The students are often divided in their responses. Some students are inclined to place a particular interpretation of Jonah closer to the center of the target than others. Allowing for these differences, I point out that no one places the answer to this question near the bullseye. As a biblical text, the story of Jonah is surely important, but our particular interpretation of it is not a matter of salvation. I also ask students questions about where various practices of faith would appear on the target. For instance, "Where would you place your beliefs about Christians drinking alcohol?" How we answer questions like these is often a matter of personal preference or convictions. Again, they do not come anywhere close to the center of what we believe. They are not important for orthodoxy or essential for salvation but personal elements of our faith.

Other issues come closer to the center. They are not the bullseye, but they surround the bullseye as "important elements." For example: *What do you believe about the inspiration of Scripture? What do you believe about baptism? What do you believe about how the Second Coming of Jesus will occur?* These kinds of questions are very important. In class, we sometimes have spirited discussions about how close some of these questions should come to the center of the target. The students typically agree that, while they are closer to the center, it would be a mistake to place them on the bullseye.

TWO TAKEAWAYS FOR CHRISTIAN CONVICTION

These exercises—especially the target exercise—help my students to realize two important truths. First, they are a reminder that not every issue is worth fighting for in the same way. I typically talk about "fighting" for truth when I walk my students through this exercise in a class I teach on Christian apologetics. Apologetics is the

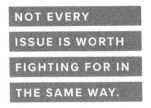
NOT EVERY ISSUE IS WORTH FIGHTING FOR IN THE SAME WAY.

discipline of defending the faith using sound reasons. In my experience, skeptics often try to undermine a person's faith by nibbling at issues that occupy the periphery of the target. I cannot count how many times I have been asked by an incredulous skeptic, "You really believe that a snake talked to a woman in some ancient garden?" The target exercise reminds me that I do not have to defend everything. Some elements of my faith are much more important than my particular interpretation of the Genesis narrative about the serpent and Eve. I encourage my students to have conversations with skeptics only about the things that are absolutely essential rather than trying to defend every square inch of the target of faith.

Second, this exercise reminds my students and us today of the dangers of what I call "epistemic legalism." "Epistemic" is just a fancy word that means "knowledge." The New Testament tells us very clearly that we cannot be saved by our own good works (Ephesians 2:8–9), and attempts to earn salvation through good works is sometimes called "legalism." Yet many who rightly reject "good works" legalism still struggle with epistemic legalism. They worry that unless they believe absolutely everything in the right way, God will reject them. They imagine God to be a cruel, celestial teacher who will greet us with a multiple-choice exam when we die. If we answer any of the questions wrongly, then he will reject us. This is just another form of legalism, in which we try to earn salvation not with good works but with perfect belief. This is not an accurate picture of God or of the gospel. Plus, it does not paint a realistic picture of ourselves. Because we are human, not one of us is capable of perfect belief. Paul reminds us that now we see things only in part in this life (1 Corinthians 13:12). We need to understand and believe what is essential and humbly ask for grace in what we might get wrong the further we move away from the bullseye. This progression naturally leads to the need for us to identify what is essential, to which we now turn.

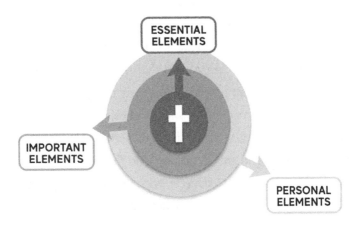

REFLECTION & DISCUSSION QUESTIONS

1. Why is it important to be able to recognize religious beliefs as either essential, important, or personal?

2. How do our personal religious backgrounds influence our essential, important, and personal beliefs?

3. Our salvation does not depend on our getting all our beliefs correct. How would you expain this to someone who didn't understand this truth?

_____

_____

_____

_____

_____

_____

4. What fundamental beliefs about God do you hold as "essential" (those that fall in the bullseye)?

_____

_____

_____

_____

_____

_____

5. Describe an experience you've had with another Christian when your essential, important, or personal beliefs did not line up and it caused conflict between you.

_____

_____

_____

_____

_____

_____

6. Pray about potential "epistemic legalism" tied to your belief system, and ask God to reveal any of this type of legalism in your life.

_____

_____

_____

_____

_____

_____

3

WHAT ARE THE ESSENTIALS OF BIBLICAL CHRISTIANITY?

Answer: The essential truths are that God exists, Jesus is Lord, Jesus is the risen Savior, and salvation is by grace and not by human effort. The essential markers of our salvation are the indwelling of the Holy Spirit and a faith that perseveres.

> And without faith it is impossible to please God, because anyone who comes to him must believe that he exists and that he rewards those who earnestly seek him.
> — Hebrews 11:6

Many elements are important to our Christian faith, and a few are actually essential (meaning that we cannot be saved without them). Some of these essential beliefs have been articulated and passed down to us in various creeds, such as the Apostles' Creed. These statements can be very helpful in identifying core Christian teachings. My goal with this chapter is not to create a new creed. Instead, I go to Scripture to identify the essential elements of the Christian faith. These elements include core doctrines we believe and an active faith by which we live. Because of this, we should expect that there are fewer of them than what we find in a traditional creed. This is a task I enter humbly and prayerfully, wanting to speak only where Scripture speaks. It is clear to me that Scripture identifies six essential elements.

1. IT IS ESSENTIAL FOR A CHRISTIAN TO BELIEVE THAT GOD EXISTS (AND TO EARNESTLY SEEK HIM).

IT MAY SEEM OBVIOUS that a person cannot be saved if they do not believe in God's existence, but we must not let what is obvious go unsaid. I remember watching a video on YouTube discussing Europe's new atheists. One particular interview was with a college student in Ireland who identified as a "Christian atheist." He had rejected the existence of God but still "respected

Jesus" enough to call himself a Christian. This is absurd. Hebrews 11:6 says, "And without faith it is impossible to please God, because anyone who comes to him must believe that he exists and that he rewards those who earnestly seek him." A person cannot please God without faith, and faith begins with the acknowledgement that God exists. Similar to this is the conviction that everything else that exists was created by God (Hebrews 11:3; see also Genesis 1:1; John 1:1–3).

You will notice that Hebrews 11:6 does not stop at mere belief in God. The verse associates belief in God with earnestly seeking him. Seeking God takes us beyond vague ideas of a deity and brings us to the personal God of Scripture. An intellectual belief in God is not enough for salvation; we must also actively orient our lives toward him. This is the kind of faith that pleases God and is rewarded by God. By faith, we must be committed to seeking God and submitting to him. James makes a similar point in James 2:17, which I quoted in Chapter 1, with a subsequent jarring point about demons.

> In the same way, faith by itself, if it is not
> accompanied by action, is dead. But someone
> will say, "You have faith; I have deeds." Show me
> your faith without deeds, and I will show you my
> faith by my deeds. You believe that there is one

God. Good! Even the demons believe that—and shudder. (James 2:17–19)

I would argue that believing in God without seeking him amounts to practical atheism. Believing without seeking is like a young married man who acknowledges his marriage yet lives every day as if he were single. Living faith is reflected in a lifestyle directed toward God (more on that below).

2. IT IS ESSENTIAL THAT A CHRISTIAN BELIEVES JESUS IS LORD.

PAUL SAYS IN ROMANS 10:9, "If you declare with your mouth, 'Jesus is Lord,' and believe in your heart that God raised him from the dead, you will be saved." The confession that Jesus is Lord was essential to Christian belief from the very beginning.[5] John 20:28 is an important passage that tells us the story of Thomas, who, upon seeing and touching the resurrected Jesus, cried out, "My Lord and my God" (John 20:28b). This simple yet shocking declaration becomes a cornerstone belief of any follower of Jesus. Biblical scholar Grant Osborne puts it this way: "At the heart of true Christian worship is the realization that Jesus is more than a mere Rabbi, more even than a Messiah. He is fully God and Lord of all."[6]

As Osborne points out, calling Jesus "Lord" is so much more than a title of respect. The Jews associated lordship with God himself. Around six thousand times in the Hebrew Scriptures (our Old Testament), God is referred to as "Lord." Even Gentiles (non-Jews) would have associated the title of Lord with the authority granted to a divine figure. This title was sometimes associated with the emperor who reigned in a "more-than-merely-human sense."[7] Therefore, when we confess Jesus is Lord, we are doing much more than merely saying that he is our "personal Lord." No, to confess that Jesus is Lord is to agree with Jesus' words to his disciples at the end of Matthew's Gospel: "All authority in heaven and on earth has been given to me" (Matthew 28:18b). Only God himself can hold all authority.

With this being said, it is also important to recognize that the belief in Jesus as Lord is deeply personal. Jesus has all authority in heaven and earth, which includes authority over our lives. This is the heart of discipleship. Paul says toward the end of his letter to the Romans, "If we live, we live for the Lord; and if we die, we die for the Lord. So, whether we live or die, we belong to the Lord" (Romans 14:8). To declare "Jesus is Lord" means that he is the center of our lives, or, as Paul puts it in another place, "I have been crucified with Christ and I no longer live, but Christ lives in me" (Galatians 2:20a). A Christian who says Jesus is Lord is not just describing something about the world; they are also describing something about their own heart. Jesus has given them—us—a new identity, a new hope, and a new purpose to live for his glory.

3. IT IS ESSENTIAL THAT A CHRISTIAN BELIEVES THAT JESUS IS THE RISEN SAVIOR.

IN THE VERSE FROM Romans 10 quoted above, it is not only the confession that Jesus is Lord that Paul associates with salvation. He adds the belief in the resurrection of Jesus from the dead as essential to salvation. Lordship and resurrection go hand in hand, not just here but also in places like Acts 2. In that passage, Peter preached the founding sermon of the church. He declared that, although Jesus had been crucified, "God has raised this Jesus to life, and we are all witnesses of it" (Acts 2:32). A few verses later, he said, "Therefore, let all Israel be assured of this: God has made this Jesus, whom you crucified, both Lord and Messiah" (Acts 2:36). It is common in the New Testament for Jesus to be called Lord. He is often called "Lord Jesus" (forty-three times) or "Lord Jesus Christ" (sixty times). Notably, these titles do not occur in the Gospels before the resurrection, but they are used extensively after it. The confession of

Jesus' lordship and the belief in his resurrection are vitally connected.

A professor of mine in graduate school put it this way: "If Jesus has risen from the dead, then nothing else matters. If Jesus has not risen from the dead, then nothing at all matters." This echoes the thought of Paul in 1 Corinthians 15. At the beginning of the chapter, Paul says he wants to remind the Corinthians of the gospel. He writes, "By this gospel you are saved" (1 Corinthians 15:2a). Then, in verses 3–8, Paul briefly explains the gospel:[8]

> For what I received I passed on to you as of first importance: that Christ died for our sins according to the Scriptures, that he was buried, that he was raised on the third day according to the Scriptures, and that he appeared to Cephas, and then to the Twelve. After that, he appeared to more than five hundred of the brothers and sisters at the same time, most of whom are still living, though some have fallen asleep. Then he appeared to James, then to all the apostles, and last of all he appeared to me also, as to one abnormally born.

These verses show us how Jesus saves us. He died as a sacrifice for our sins, and that death was followed by a physical resurrection. Later in the chapter, Paul makes a blunt point: "If there is no resurrection of the dead, then not even Christ has been raised. And if Christ has not been raised, our preaching is useless and so is your faith" (1 Corinthians 15:13–14). Believing in Jesus' resurrection is essential for salvation because without the resurrection there is no salvation. Without the resurrection, Jesus' death on the cross was of no consequence, and we are still in our sins (1 Corinthians 15:17). The good news, however, is that Jesus is both our risen Savior and our Lord. The resurrection is the truth that revolutionized the world and continues to transform lives.

4. IT IS ESSENTIAL THAT A CHRISTIAN IS SAVED BY GRACE THROUGH FAITH AND NOT BY HUMAN EFFORT.

IN EPHESIANS 2:8–9, PAUL says, "For it is by grace you have been saved, through faith—and this is not from yourselves, it is the gift of God—not by works, so that no one can boast." Grace is the *means* of our salvation. We are not able to save ourselves. Even though we deserve death and separation from God because of sin, salvation is an unearned gift (see also Romans 6:23). Faith is the *agency* of our

GRACE IS THE MEANS OF OUR SALVATION. WE ARE NOT ABLE TO SAVE OURSELVES.

salvation. We are not saved *by* faith; we are saved *through* faith.

One way we can understand this is to think about how we are physically alive right now. We are living *by* oxygen. Without oxygen, we would suffocate and die, but we are also living *through* our lungs. All the oxygen in the world will do us no good without properly functioning lungs. So we are saved by God's grace and receive that grace through faith.

Paul makes it emphatically clear in the above verses that our good works do not save us. As he points out in the following verse (Ephesians 2:10), we are saved *to do good works*, but we cannot earn our salvation *by good works*. Attempting to be "good enough" to earn our salvation denies the sufficient work of Jesus on the cross. This is why Paul declares to the Galatian Christians that they have been bewitched into following a non-gospel that denies grace (Galatians 3:1). He summarizes, "I do not set aside the grace of God, for if righteousness could be gained through the law, Christ died for nothing!" (Galatians 2:21).

Denying grace seemed to get Paul incredibly angry. It got Jesus angry too. In the Gospels, Jesus regularly rebuked the Pharisees for their hypocrisy and public displays of righteousness. Ironically, it was the tax collectors, the prostitutes, and other sinners who were repenting and believing in Jesus (Matthew 21:32). The self-righteousness of the religious leaders was actually keeping them from believing and thus from being saved. In the same way, our salvation is dependent on our trust in the work of Jesus and not in our own works of righteousness. Paul reminds us of this: "You see, at just the right time, when we were still powerless, Christ died for the ungodly" (Romans 5:6). This is good news! It is only upon discovering our own powerlessness that we are truly ready to be saved.

5. IT IS ESSENTIAL THAT A CHRISTIAN BE BORN AGAIN BY THE HOLY SPIRIT.

ONE NIGHT, JESUS WAS approached by a religious leader named Nicodemus. Like many people today, Nicodemus was not only curious but also cautious about Jesus. Nicodemus asked Jesus a question about his identity, and in Jesus' typical style, he answered the question indirectly: "Very truly I tell you, no one can see the kingdom of God unless they are born again" (John 3:3). We can easily understand why Nicodemus was confused by the answer: *Born again? How does that work? How is a fully grown man born again?*

Jesus responded, "Very truly I tell you, no one can enter the kingdom of God unless they are born of water and the Spirit. Flesh gives birth to flesh, but the Spirit gives birth to spirit" (John 3:5–6). It is likely that Jesus was calling to mind the words we find in Ezekiel 36:25–28, in which God promised a time when he would renew his people and place his Spirit within them. Jesus was telling Nicodemus the amazing news that the time anticipated by Ezekiel had arrived in him! God has granted us a new life and a new place in his kingdom by being born again by the Holy Spirit.

I used to ask students in one of my freshman Bible classes at the beginning of the semester, "What really makes a person a Christian?" Sometimes, I put it another way: "How do we know if a person is a Christian?" I would get a variety of answers. Often, answers would gravitate toward behaviors typical of a Christian: a Christian goes to church, a Christian engages in disciplines like prayer or Bible reading, a Christian acts in ways that are distinct from the world. The expectation implicit to these responses is that being a Christian does change the way a person lives their life (e.g., Ephesians 4:1–2). Yet to Jesus what matters for salvation is new life in the Spirit. It's not just important but essential to salvation. The distinguishing mark of a Christian is that the Holy Spirit has taken up residence in their life to make them a new person.

We observe this in the book of Acts when the church was born through the power of the Holy Spirit working through the apostles (Acts 1:8). New believers were promised the gift of the Holy Spirit upon their repentance and baptism (Acts 2:38). Paul also emphasizes the new life we experience in the Spirit in Ephesians when he says that we are included in Christ when we believe the gospel, adding that believers are "marked in him with a seal, the promised Holy Spirit, who is a deposit guaranteeing our inheritance until the redemption of those who are God's possession—to the praise of his glory" (Ephesians 1:13b–14). Paul makes the same point in Romans, that "if anyone does not have the Spirit of Christ, they do not belong to Christ" (Romans 8:9b). He goes on to say that even though we are subject to death because of our sin, the Spirit gives us life (Romans 8:10–11), and we are now children of God by the Spirit (Romans 8:14–17). John expresses the point too: "This is how we know that we live in him and he in us: He has given us of his Spirit" (1 John 4:13).

As we said in the previous point, we are saved only by God's grace. It is also true that we experience new life only through the Holy Spirit's work within us. God does call us to pursue righteousness and godliness with our lives, but this pursuit is *in response* to being born again by the Spirit (see Ephesians 2:10; 4:1). A life that is lived independently of the power and influence of the Holy Spirit is not a Christian life. On the other hand, a life that has been reborn of the Spirit will produce righteous fruit (Galatians 5:22–25) and gifts to be used for building others up (1 Corinthians 12:7–30).

6. IT IS ESSENTIAL THAT A CHRISTIAN PERSEVERE IN A FAITHFUL FAITH.

THE BOOK OF HEBREWS was written to a group of Christians who were growing weary in their faith because they had encountered hardship and opposition as a result of their faith. Thomas Long summarizes their situation this way: "Tired of walking the walk, many of them are considering taking a walk, leaving the community and falling away from the faith."[9] Hebrews was written in order to encourage its recipients to persevere in their faith. The author warns them to "pay the most careful attention, therefore, to what we have heard, so that we do not drift away" (Hebrews 2:1). Then, in the next chapter, the author challenges them to encourage each other daily because "we have come to share in Christ, if indeed we hold our original conviction firmly to the very end" (Hebrews 3:14). Later, in Hebrews 6, the author exhorts them to not "become lazy, but to imitate those who through faith and patience inherit what has been promised" (Hebrews 6:12). Then he says to remember the example of Jesus, "who endured such opposition from sinners, so that [they would] not grow weary and lose heart" (Hebrews 12:3). The message of Hebrews is clear: believers must persevere in their faith, not giving up but being resolute in their commitment to Christ.

Perseverance is a common theme not just in Hebrews but also throughout the New Testament. Jesus tells us a parable comparing his kingdom to a farmer who went out to sow his seed. Some of the farmer's seed falls on rocky ground. The plant sprouts up quickly, but then it withers just as quickly. Jesus says this is the person who believes for a little while, but falls away during testing (Luke 8:13). The book of James puts it this way: "Blessed is the one who perseveres under trial because, having stood the test, that person will receive the crown of life that the Lord has promised to those who love him" (James 1:12). Paul also regularly talks about the need for perseverance and endurance. Perseverance in the midst of suffering is essential for a mature faith (Romans 5:3–5; see also 2 Corinthians 1:6; 1 Thessalonians 1:3–4).

A living faith perseveres. Believers express faith through a repentant lifestyle (Hebrews 10:26; Galatians 5:19–21). It is easy in this world to gradually "drift away" from our faith, sometimes because of hardships, pain, or suffering. Some of us know from experience that faith can become difficult

A LIVING FAITH PERSEVERES.

to maintain in those moments. More often, though, we drift because we simply get distracted or sidetracked by all of the other issues of life and our commitment to Jesus just withers from inattention. Then, other times, our sin deceives us (Hebrews 3:13). For all these reasons, we must remain actively and intentionally engaged in the life of the church each and every day to encourage our brothers and sisters in the faith (see Hebrews 10:19–25).

REFLECTION & DISCUSSION QUESTIONS

1. Review your answer to question 4 in Chapter 2 (page 38). Now that you've read this section, how has your list of essential truths changed?

_____

_____

_____

_____

_____

2. What is the difference, practically speaking, in intellectually believing *in God* and *seeking after him* in your life?

_____

_____

_____

_____

_____

_____

3. If someone asked you to describe how Jesus saves us, how would you explain it?

_____

_____

_____

_____

_____

_____

_____

4. What is the basis of your confidence that the Holy Spirit lives in you? Explain.

_____

_____

_____

_____

_____

_____

5. What events in our lives can challenge our perseverance in having a faithful faith?

_____

_____

_____

_____

_____

_____

_____

6. What are some strategies that might encourage us to persevere in our faith? The verses explored in the sixth point may be helpful in thinking through these strategies.

_____

_____

_____

_____

_____

_____

4

HOW SHOULD WE TREAT ELEMENTS OF OUR FAITH THAT ARE NOT ESSENTIAL?

Answer: Important but secondary elements of the faith are vital. Our faithfulness to God requires us to seek and pursue them, even as we acknowledge that our salvation may not be dependent on getting them right.

He began to speak boldly in the synagogue.
When Priscilla and Aquila heard him, they
invited him to their home and explained to
him the way of God more adequately.
— Acts 18:26

Two circumstances from my early days in ministry come to mind when I think about the question of this chapter. In one circumstance, I had just finished teaching a Bible study at the small church I was pastoring on the book of Revelation where the question of the rapture had come up. The issue of the rapture divides many believers. I do not personally believe that the Bible teaches the rapture. I explained to the class that belief in the rapture is a relatively new belief among Christians and those who use biblical passages to support the rapture misinterpret those passages. Perhaps you agree with me. Perhaps you disagree. Well, a woman in the class very strongly disagreed. In fact, she was alarmed! She just could not understand how a person could be a Christian, let alone a minister, and not believe in *the rapture*. To her, the issue was so important that she felt she could no longer worship with our church.

In another circumstance, I was meeting with a woman who was thinking about joining our church after visiting for many months. She had some questions about what we believed as a church, especially with regard to baptism. I explained to her what Scripture had to say about baptism and why our church was committed to believer's baptism for the remission of sins. She asked me whether or not she could be saved without being baptized. Personally, I really do not like this question: it turns baptism into a "have to" instead of a "get to."

I told her that God's grace is what saves us. Baptism is our act of obedience in which we *get to* publicly commit ourselves to a covenant relationship with him. She was disappointed at my response, or should I say her interpretation of my answer disappointed her. To her, if baptism is not "essential," then there is really no point in getting baptized.

These two stories represent two common mistakes we sometimes make with non-essential beliefs. We tend to either make them essential to the point that we condemn anyone who does not hold our belief or we make our beliefs unimportant and not worthy of our concern. The Renew.org Network Leaders' Faith Statement about "Essential, Important, and Personal Elements" avoids both of these errors: *important* but secondary elements of the faith are vital but non-essential to salvation. That is, our faithfulness to God requires us to seek and pursue them, even as we acknowledge that our salvation may not be dependent on getting them right.

IMPORTANT BUT SECONDARY ELEMENTS OF THE FAITH ARE VITAL BUT NON-ESSENTIAL TO SALVATION.

Three New Testament stories in particular help us to know how we should treat non-essential elements of our faith.

STORY #1: THE WOMAN AT THE WELL

In John 4, Jesus had a remarkable conversation with a Samaritan woman while at a well in the middle of the day. This conversation was a violation of several social norms. In those days, a respected teacher would never have a private conversation with a woman, especially if the teacher was Jewish and the woman was a hated Samaritan. None of that mattered to Jesus. He simply saw a woman in desperate need of "living water." In the midst of their conversation, the woman asked Jesus what appears to be a peculiar question about the proper place to worship: Should people worship in Jerusalem or in Samaria? While this may seem a strange question to us, this was an important theological dispute in this woman's community. She was eager to have Jesus settle the argument. Jesus answered this way:

> "Woman," Jesus replied, "believe me, a time is coming when you will worship the Father neither on this mountain nor in Jerusalem. You Samaritans worship what you do not know; we worship what we do know, for salvation is from the Jews. Yet a time is coming and has now come when the true worshipers will worship the Father in the Spirit and in truth, for they are the kind of worshipers the

Father seeks. God is spirit, and his worshipers must worship in the Spirit and in truth." (John 4:21–24)

Notice what Jesus did here. He answered her question by redirecting her to the heart of the issue. It is not *where* you worship that ultimately matters. It is *how* you worship.

Jesus' example instructs us on how to handle important but non-essential issues. He did not dismiss her question as unimportant, but he did direct her to a deeper issue and a more important truth than what she had considered to be of utmost importance. This is the case with many of our important beliefs. It is not that these beliefs are unimportant, but there is sometimes a deeper issue that we should consider has a higher priority. Revisiting one of the examples above, the woman in my ministry had asked a question about baptism. It was an important question, but her concerns about baptism revealed the deeper issue of obedience and submission to Jesus as Lord. When we understand the joys of following Jesus and the requirements of discipleship on our lives, we stop debating baptism. Instead, it becomes a gift in which we get to partake. The essential issue of Jesus' lordship takes precedence over the non-essential— yet important—role of baptism.

STORY #2: APOLLOS

We can learn something about how to treat non-essential elements of the faith from the story of Apollos as well. We first meet Apollos in Acts 18. Luke describes him as a Jew from Alexandria, who was "a learned man, with a thorough knowledge of the Scriptures" (Acts 18:24b). The text goes on to say that "he had been instructed in the way of the Lord, and he spoke with great fervor and taught about Jesus accurately, though he knew only the baptism of John" (Acts 18:25). Apollos seemed to know what was essential and what was non-essential but important. He taught about Jesus accurately and with passion, but he still needed further instruction on the important issue of baptism. The very next verse tells us that Priscilla and Aquila, leaders in the church at Ephesus, took him into their home and "explained to him the way of God more adequately" (Acts 18:26b). Priscilla and Aquila could have condemned Apollos for his incomplete knowledge. A well-educated and articulate person like Apollos could have responded with pride or hostility at his being corrected. Thankfully—because of Priscilla and Aquila's careful instruction and Apollos's willingness to be taught—he went on to become a very important leader in the church at Corinth.

This story teaches us about the importance of what Paul calls "growing in the knowledge of God"

(Colossians 1:10). There is always more to learn, and we should be very careful not to rest content with incomplete or elementary knowledge with regard to our faith (see Hebrews 5:11–6:3). This is the way our faith becomes stunted and fruitless. When I teach high school students, I often tell them to care enough about their faith to be curious about it. Develop the regular discipline of studying Scripture; discover Christian authors who can help you to grow in your knowledge of God; and place yourself under the instruction of persons who are more mature in their faith. Apollos provides for us a model of a person who was humble enough to be taught and passionate enough to want to learn more. He knew the essentials, but he wanted to know more. He cared enough about Jesus that he wanted to follow him even more accurately. The important elements of our faith provide an invitation to continue learning and growing.

STORY #3: AN EARNEST FATHER

THE THIRD STORY IS found in Mark 9. In this chapter, we read about a father's anguish for his son who had been possessed by an evil spirit from childhood. The spirit regularly sent the boy into convulsions, putting his life in danger. Jesus' disciples could not drive out the demon, so the man came to Jesus and asked, "If you can do anything, take pity on us and help us" (Mark 9:22b).

Jesus responded by telling him that "everything is possi-

I DO BELIEVE;
HELP ME
OVERCOME MY
UNBELIEF!

ble for one who believes" (Mark 9:23b). The father did not have to think very long for his reply: "Immediately the boy's father exclaimed, 'I do believe; help me overcome my unbelief!'" (Mark 9:24).

I have always thought this was one of the most honest verses in the entire New Testament. The father believed, yet he recognized that his belief was not perfect. His belief was not without questions, not without some shadow of doubt, not without uncertainty. He was crying out not only for Jesus to heal his son but also for Jesus to heal his belief.

Many Christians (and non-Christians) labor under the assumption that all true beliefs require absolute certainty. I have personally witnessed this assumption turn toxic in a disciple's life. Because they cannot satisfactorily arrive at absolute certainty, their faith turns to despair. Sometimes this leads to nagging questions concerning whether or not God can accept them. At other times, this leads to the questioner's rejection of faith in God altogether. It is important for us to notice that Jesus does not rebuke the man for his lack of perfect belief. Instead, he dramatically heals his son. The lesson that we learn from this man is that we can honestly and prayerfully take our questions and our doubts to Jesus.

We all struggle with clarity and understanding on all sorts of issues related to God and faith. As I mentioned in Chapter 2, many of us labor under the burden of epistemic legalism. This father gives us all hope. Learn this prayer from this unnamed yet earnest father: *I do believe; help me overcome my unbelief.*

REFLECTION & DISCUSSION QUESTIONS

1. Describe a time when you experienced someone, maybe even yourself, putting important truths into the essential category.

_____

_____

_____

_____

_____

_____

2. What are some examples of essential beliefs that you uphold? Have they changed over time?

_____

_____

_____

_____

_____

3. How could mixing up essential truths, important truths, and personal preferences turn Christians against one another? What advice would you give to someone who is mixing them up and causing division?

4. Why is it important to gain knowledge in order to understand and then commit to the essential truths of Scripture?

5. The father with the demon-possessed child told Jesus, "I do believe; help me overcome my unbelief." Similarly, what is a question or doubt that you want to take to Jesus?

_____

_____

_____

_____

_____

_____

6. In what areas of your faith are you wanting to gain more knowledge in order to determine whether they should fit into the essential, important, or personal elements?

_____

_____

_____

_____

_____

_____

5

HOW SHOULD WE TREAT THOSE WHO DISAGREE WITH US?

Answer: When we disagree about matters of personal preference, we are to respond to each other with grace and truth. We are never at liberty to express our freedom in a way that causes others to stumble in sin. In all things, we want to show understanding, kindness, and love.

Accept the one whose faith is weak, without quarreling over disputable matters.
— Romans 14:1

Up to this point, we have addressed beliefs that are essential for salvation, as well as how to approach beliefs that are important for our discipleship but are not core, essential issues. This chapter goes into detail on the third category of beliefs, which I introduced above. I call these beliefs "preferences" or "matters of personal opinion." Returning to the target illustration from Chapter 2, these beliefs are typically near the outer edge of the target. They are important enough to be on the target, but not critical enough to be near the center. It is my observation that, even though these preferences are not what we call "bullseye beliefs," they do often become the center of many of our arguments and lead to defensiveness. The further we get from the center of the target, the more likely we are to argue with those who disagree with us. These personal preferences become the beliefs that distinguish us and separate us from others. This can cause conflict.

This tendency should not really surprise us. For instance, the resurrection of Jesus, as part of the gospel, is a well-established and essential belief within the Christian community. If I met a person who did not believe in the resurrection but claimed to be a Christian, I would not only dispute their belief about the resurrection but I would also dispute their claim to be a Christian. By contrast, consider beliefs about methods of worship. These beliefs are on the target, but they exist as personal preferences on the outer edge of the target. Hopefully it would never occur to someone to question another person's salvation because they have a different preference in worship style. Unfortunately, however, I've observed that many more churches have split over worship preferences than over beliefs regarding inerrancy or the resurrection. My point is this: unless we are committed to hanging out only with people who agree with us on everything, we will have to figure out how to respond to people who disagree with us, especially with regard to our personal preferences. Fortunately, Scripture provides us some help.

THE EXAMPLE OF JESUS

First, let us consider the example of Jesus himself. John 1:14 says, "The Word became flesh and made his dwelling among us. We have seen his glory, the glory of the one and only Son, who came from the Father, full of grace and truth." This is a breathtaking verse about the identity of Jesus, but for our purposes, I want to focus only on the last phrase: Jesus came into the world "full of grace and truth."

Grace and truth serve as twin anchor points for Jesus' ministry. Initially we may think that grace and truth oppose each other. Truth, we assume, is unbending and rigid. Grace, on the other hand, is flexible and forgiving. Jesus demonstrates, however, that rather than opposing each other, grace and truth are necessary complements to one another. Grace without truth becomes flimsy and cheap; truth without grace becomes oppressive and cold. In Jesus, we observe that perfect balance. He came bringing truth and light into a dark world (John 1:4–5; 3:19; 8:12; 9:5). Jesus was passionate about truth. The word *truth* occurs twenty-eight times just in the book of John, but this truth was not oppressive. No, the truth Jesus introduced to the world brought us the opportunity for grace and forgiveness (John 3:16–21).

Jesus' lifestyle of grace and truth provides a lesson for us about how to engage with people who disagree with us. We must remain committed to truth and vigilant about accepting ideas that are false or harmful to our faith. This is the heart of Paul's encouragement to "take captive every thought" (2 Corinthians 10:5b). Discipleship calls on us to question the conventional wisdom of the world (1 Corinthians 1:20–31), while watching our lives and doctrine closely (1 Timothy 4:16). We also recognize that the truth of the gospel is truth about the grace we have received in Christ.

Jesus had some very harsh words for people who expected to be forgiven yet were unwilling to show forgiveness to others (Matthew 6:14–15; 18:21–35). I once heard a Christian author repeat a proverb he heard growing up: "It is no use cutting off a man's nose and then asking that he smell a rose." He was making a point about the necessity of truth seasoned with grace. If we declare the truth about Jesus with hostility and without any grace or forgiveness, it will be impossible to convince a person that Jesus sacrificially loves them and wants to save them from their sin.[10]

Paul models the difficult balance between grace and truth in 2 Timothy 2:1–25: He begins the chapter by exhorting Timothy to "be strong in the grace that is in Christ Jesus" (2 Timothy 2:1). To Paul, being strong in grace requires strong teaching and commitment to truth. He tells Timothy to entrust this teaching to reliable people who can teach others (2 Timothy 2:2). Later, he tells Timothy to remember the essentials of the faith (2 Timothy 2:8) and to warn people about "quarreling about words" (2 Timothy 2:14) and "godless chatter" (2 Timothy 2:16). Godless chatter is so dangerous because it works like a disease that spreads through a community, and if left unchecked, it may even result in the destruction of faith (2 Timothy 2:16–18). The chapter closes with Paul warning Timothy to avoid "foolish and stupid arguments" (2 Timothy 2:23). Paul is warning Timothy about getting caught up in arguing about issues that are unimportant. Instead, Timothy should gently instruct his opponents "in the hope that God will grant them repentance leading them to a knowledge of the truth" (2 Timothy 2:25).

Do you see grace mixed with truth in these instructions? Commit yourself to the truth and to sound teaching. Do not give in to foolish arguments. Instead, gently instruct your opponents in the hopes that they will arrive at the truth. We should also add this note: We may not always identify with Timothy in this text. Often we are the ones who need correction and teaching. Grace and truth require that we have the humility to receive this instruction.

So the first way to answer the question of how to treat those with whom we disagree in the body of Christ, then, is this: The manner in which Jesus came into the world is also the way that we conduct ourselves in the world—full of grace and truth. The second answer to the question has to do with my kids and their shoes.

KIDS AND SHOES

ONE OF THE CONSTANT battles my wife and I fight in our house involves kids and shoes. We remind our kids to pick up their shoes and put them away after they have taken them off. Way too often, however, my kids will come in the door and leave their shoes wherever they happen to take them off. (I must confess that it is not just the kids who have this habit!)

The floor of our kitchen and living room quickly becomes a labyrinth of discarded flip-flops and tennis shoes. I explain to them that there are two problems with leaving their shoes out. First, it just looks messy, and second, it is a safety hazard. They—*we*—create an obstacle course of shoes this way, just inviting someone to trip over them, especially at night when it is hard to see. We remove the potential tripping hazard by putting our shoes where they belong, and this is a way of saying that we care about one another. This is true about shoes in the middle of the floor, but it is also true about beliefs that are a matter of personal preference. Let me explain.

Paul talks about the idea of personal preferences in faith in Romans 14 (see also 1 Corinthians 8). Paul's exhortation to the Romans begins, "Accept the one whose faith is weak, without quarreling over *disputable matters*" (Romans 14:1). Apparently, members of this Christian community had not yet grown into maturity in their faith. Paul instructs them to accept these people who were young in their faith rather than quarrel with them about disputable matters. John Stott, in his commentary on Romans, says that to accept someone means "to welcome [them] into one's fellowship and into one's heart. It implies the warmth and kindness of genuine love."[11] Instead of judging one another on these matters, Paul tells the Roman Christians, "Make up your mind not to put any stumbling block or obstacle in the way of a brother or sister" (Romans 14:13b). In other words, do not use your convictions on disputable matters to destroy the community or destroy your brother or sister's faith. Instead, "make every effort to do what leads to peace and to mutual edification" (Romans 14:19).

DO NOT USE YOUR CONVICTIONS ON DISPUTABLE MATTERS TO DESTROY THE COMMUNITY.

The principle is that we love each other enough to willingly remove hazardous obstacles to faith for those who might not share our personal convictions on disputable matters. This does not mean that we compromise on the essentials of our faith; neither does it mean that we stop caring about those important beliefs that are not essential. This principle of accepting those with weak faith means that in matters of personal preference we prioritize love for each other and the unity of our community over "being right."

Let me offer an example to illustrate the point further. The matter of drinking alcohol has long been a source of debate among Christians. Some Christians believe that drinking alcohol is permissible as long as a person avoids drunkenness. Other Christians believe that because drinking alcohol so consistently leads to abuse, it is not permissible for a Christian to drink any alcohol. I believe that this issue falls into the category of personal preference, what Paul calls "disputable matters." A person's position on drinking alcohol does not come anywhere close to a bullseye belief. So how does the Romans 14 principle help us to approach the issue?

First, we are committed to loving those who disagree with us and to protecting the unity of the body of Christ. Disagreements do not exempt us from the command to love one another (John 13:34–35; Romans 12:10; 13:8). It is possible and necessary to disagree without condemning one another on matters like these. Second, our love for each other means that we should be ready to forgo our personal preferences for the sake of *the weaker Christian*. I may believe that I have freedom to consume alcohol, but if my drinking alcohol is a potential stumbling block for someone in my community, love compels me to submit my freedom to their spiritual need (see 1 Corinthians 8:9). This does not mean that we cannot talk about the issue among those who disagree, but we should not allow disagreement on the issue to hinder anyone's faith. As the Renew.org Network Leaders' Faith Statement says, "We are never at liberty to express our freedom in a way that causes others to stumble in sin. In all things, we want to show understanding, kindness, and love."

> IN ALL THINGS, WE WANT TO SHOW UNDERSTANDING, KINDNESS, AND LOVE.

REFLECTION & DISCUSSION QUESTIONS

1. What are some examples in which your faith tradition or church background affected your personal preferences?

_____

_____

_____

_____

_____

2. In this chapter, I describe grace and truth from the Bible. Can you think of any stories from Scripture that illustrate grace and truth?

_____

_____

_____

_____

_____

_____

3. Do you struggle more with showing grace
   or showing truth? How would you explain to
   someone the importance of both?

_____

_____

_____

_____

_____

4. Can you give a personal example of a time
   you received truth without grace or grace
   without truth?

_____

_____

_____

_____

_____

_____

5. Read 2 Timothy 2:22–26. Summarize in your own words the type of person who Paul is calling us to be. What are the things that get in the way of being this type of person?

_____

_____

_____

_____

_____

_____

6. Share an experience you've had with a wise Christian who understood and practiced what Paul describes in Romans 14 about disputable matters.

_____

_____

_____

_____

_____

_____

APPENDIX A

BOOK RECOMMENDATIONS FOR FURTHER STUDY

Rebecca McLaughlin, *Confronting Christianity: 12 Hard Questions for the World's Largest Religion* (Wheaton: Crossway, 2019).

Mark Moore, *Core 52: A Fifteen-Minute Daily Guide to Build Your Bible IQ in a Year* (Colorado Springs: WaterBrook, 2019).

Ben Myers, *The Apostles' Creed: A Guide to the Ancient Catechism* (Bellingham: Lexham Press, 2018).

C. S. Lewis, *Mere Christianity* (New York: HarperOne, 2015).

N. T. Wright, *Simply Christian: Why Christianity Makes Sense* (New York: HarperCollins, 2006).

APPENDIX B

RENEW.ORG NETWORK LEADERS' VALUES AND FAITH STATEMENTS

Mission: We Renew the Teachings of Jesus to Fuel Disciple Making

Vision: A collaborative network equipping millions of disciples, disciple makers, and church planters among all ethnicities.

SEVEN VALUES

RENEWAL IN THE BIBLE and in history follows a discernible outline that can be summarized by seven key elements. We champion these elements as our core values. They are listed in a sequential pattern that is typical of renewal, and it all starts with God.

1. *Renewing by God's Spirit.* We believe that God is the author of renewal and that he invites us to access and join him through prayer and fasting for the Holy Spirit's work of renewal.

2. *Following God's Word.* We learn the ways of God with lasting clarity and conviction by trusting God's Word and what it teaches as the objective foundation for renewal and life.

3. *Surrendering to Jesus' Lordship.* The gospel teaches us that Jesus is Messiah (King) and Lord. He calls everyone to salvation (in eternity) and discipleship (in this life) through a faith commitment that is expressed in repentance, confession, and baptism. Repentance and surrender to Jesus as Lord is the never-ending cycle for life in Jesus' kingdom, and it is empowered by the Spirit.

4. *Championing disciple making.* Jesus personally gave us his model of disciple making, which he demonstrated with his disciples. Those same principles from the life of Jesus should be utilized as we make disciples today and champion discipleship as the core mission of the local church.

5. *Loving like Jesus.* Jesus showed us the true meaning of love and taught us that sacrificial love is the

distinguishing character trait of true disciples (and true renewal). Sacrificial love is the foundation for our relationships both in the church and in the world.

6. *Living in holiness.* Just as Jesus lived differently from the world, the people in his church will learn to live differently than the world. Even when it is difficult, we show that God's kingdom is an alternative kingdom to the world.

7. *Leading courageously.* God always uses leaders in renewal who live by a prayerful, risk-taking faith. Renewal will be led by bold and courageous leaders—who make disciples, plant churches, and create disciple making movements.

TEN FAITH STATEMENTS

We believe that Jesus Christ is Lord. We are a group of church leaders inviting others to join the theological and disciple making journey described below. We want to trust and follow Jesus Christ to the glory of God the Father in the power of the Holy Spirit. We are committed to *restoring* the kingdom vision of Jesus and the apostles, especially the *message* of Jesus' gospel, the *method* of disciple making he showed us, and the *model* of what a community of his disciples, at their best, can become.

We live in a time when cultural pressures are forcing us to face numerous difficulties and complexities in following God. Many are losing their resolve. We trust that God is gracious and forgives the errors of those with genuine faith in his Son, but our desire is to be faithful in all things.

Our focus is disciple making, which is both reaching lost people (evangelism) and bringing people to maturity (sanctification). We seek to be a movement of disciple making leaders who make disciples and other disciple makers. We want to renew existing churches and help plant multiplying churches.

1. *God's Word.* We believe God gave us the sixty-six books of the Bible to be received as the inspired, authoritative, and infallible Word of God for salvation and life. The documents of Scripture come to us as diverse literary and historical writings. Despite their complexities, they can be understood, trusted, and followed. We want to do the hard work of wrestling to understand Scripture in order to obey God. We want to avoid the errors of interpreting Scripture through the sentimental lens of our feelings and opinions or through a complex re-interpretation of plain meanings so that the Bible says what our culture says. Ours is a time for both clear thinking and courage. Because the Holy Spirit inspired all sixty-six books, we honor Jesus' Lordship by submitting our lives to all that God has for us in them.

Psalm 1; 119; Deuteronomy 4:1–6; 6:1–9;
2 Chronicles 34; Nehemiah 8; Matthew 5:1–7:28;
15:6–9; John 12:44–50; Matthew 28:19; Acts 2:42;
17:10–11; 2 Timothy 3:16–4:4; 1 Peter 1:20–21.

2. *Christian convictions.* We believe the Scriptures reveal three distinct elements of the faith: *essential* elements which are necessary for salvation; *important* elements which are to be pursued so that we faithfully follow Christ; and *personal* elements or opinion. The gospel is *essential.* Every person who is indwelt and sealed by God's Holy Spirit because of their faith in the gospel is a brother or a sister in Christ. *Important* but secondary elements of the faith are vital. Our faithfulness to God requires us to seek and pursue them, even as we acknowledge that our salvation may not be dependent on getting them right. And thirdly, there are personal matters of opinion, disputable areas where God gives us personal freedom. But we are never at liberty to express our freedom in a way that causes others to stumble in sin. In all things, we want to show understanding, kindness, and love.

1 Corinthians 15:1–8; Romans 1:15–17;
Galatians 1:6–9; 2 Timothy 2:8; Ephesians 1:13–14;
4:4–6; Romans 8:9; 1 Corinthians 12:13;
1 Timothy 4:16; 2 Timothy 3:16–4:4;

Matthew 15:6–9; Acts 20:32; 1 Corinthians 11:1–2;
1 John 2:3–4; 2 Peter 3:14–16; Romans 14:1–23.

3. *The gospel.* We believe God created all things and made human beings in his image, so that we could enjoy a relationship with him and each other. But we lost our way, through Satan's influence. We are now spiritually dead, separated from God. Without his help, we gravitate toward sin and self-rule. The gospel is God's good news of reconciliation. It was promised to Abraham and David and revealed in Jesus' life, ministry, teaching, and sacrificial death on the cross. The gospel is the saving action of the triune God. The Father sent the Son into the world to take on human flesh and redeem us. Jesus came as the promised Messiah of the Old Testament. He ushered in the kingdom of God, died for our sins according to Scripture, was buried, and was raised on the third day. He defeated sin and death and ascended to heaven. He is seated at the right hand of God as Lord and he is coming back for his disciples. Through the Spirit, we are transformed and sanctified. God will raise everyone for the final judgment. Those who trusted and followed Jesus by faith will not experience punishment for their sins and separation from God in hell. Instead, we will join together with God in the renewal of all things in the consummated kingdom. We will live

together in the new heaven and new earth where we will glorify God and enjoy him forever.

> *Genesis 1–3; Romans 3:10–12; 7:8–25;*
> *Genesis 12:1–3; Galatians 3:6–9; Isaiah 11:1–4;*
> *2 Samuel 7:1–16; Micah 5:2–4; Daniel 2:44–45;*
> *Luke 1:33; John 1:1–3; Matthew 4:17;*
> *1 Corinthians 15:1–8; Acts 1:11; 2:36; 3:19–21;*
> *Colossians 3:1; Matthew 25:31–32; Revelation 21:1ff;*
> *Romans 3:21–26.*

4. *Faithful faith.* We believe that people are saved by grace through faith. The gospel of Jesus' kingdom calls people to both salvation and discipleship—no exceptions, no excuses. Faith is more than mere intellectual agreement or emotional warmth toward God. It is living and active; faith is surrendering our self-rule to the rule of God through Jesus in the power of the Spirit. We surrender by trusting and following Jesus as both Savior and Lord in all things. Faith includes allegiance, loyalty, and faithfulness to him.

> *Ephesians 2:8–9; Mark 8:34–38; Luke 14:25–35;*
> *Romans 1:3, 5; 16:25–26; Galatians 2:20;*
> *James 2:14–26; Matthew 7:21–23; Galatians 4:19;*
> *Matthew 28:19–20; 2 Corinthians 3:3, 17–18;*
> *Colossians 1:28.*

5. *New birth.* God so loved the world that he gave his one and only Son, that whoever believes in him shall not perish but have eternal life. To believe in Jesus means we trust and follow him as both Savior and Lord. When we commit to trust and follow Jesus, we express this faith by repenting from sin, confessing his name, and receiving baptism by immersion in water. Baptism, as an expression of faith, is for the remission of sins. We uphold baptism as the normative means of entry into the life of discipleship. It marks our commitment to regularly die to ourselves and rise to live for Christ in the power of the Holy Spirit. We believe God sovereignly saves as he sees fit, but we are bound by Scripture to uphold this teaching about surrendering to Jesus in faith through repentance, confession, and baptism.

> *1 Corinthians 8:6; John 3:1–9; 3:16–18; 3:19–21; Luke 13:3–5; 24:46–47; Acts 2:38; 3:19; 8:36–38; 16:31–33; 17:30; 20:21; 22:16; 26:20; Galatians 3:26–27; Romans 6:1–4; 10:9–10; 1 Peter 3:21; Romans 2:25–29; 2 Chronicles 30:17–19; Matthew 28:19–20; Galatians 2:20; Acts 18:24–26.*

6. *Holy Spirit.* We believe God's desire is for everyone to be saved and come to the knowledge of the truth. Many hear the gospel but do not believe it because they

are blinded by Satan and resist the pull of the Holy Spirit. We encourage everyone to listen to the Word and let the Holy Spirit convict them of their sin and draw them into a relationship with God through Jesus. We believe that when we are born again and indwelt by the Holy Spirit, we are to live as people who are filled, empowered, and led by the Holy Spirit. This is how we walk with God and discern his voice. A prayerful life, rich in the Holy Spirit, is fundamental to true discipleship and living in step with the kingdom reign of Jesus. We seek to be a prayerful, Spirit-led fellowship.

> *1 Timothy 2:4; John 16:7–11; Acts 7:51;*
> *1 John 2:20, 27; John 3:5; Ephesians 1:13–14;*
> *5:18; Galatians 5:16–25; Romans 8:5–11;*
> *Acts 1:14; 2:42; 6:6; 9:40; 12:5; 13:3; 14:23; 20:36;*
> *2 Corinthians 3:3.*

7. *Disciple making.* We believe the core mission of the local church is making disciples of Jesus Christ— it is God's plan "A" to redeem the world and manifest the reign of his kingdom. We want to be disciples who make disciples because of our love for God and others. We personally seek to become more and more like Jesus through his Spirit so that Jesus would live through us. To help us focus on Jesus, his sacrifice on the cross, our unity in him, and his coming return, we typically share

communion in our weekly gatherings. We desire the fruits of biblical disciple making which are disciples who live and love like Jesus and "go" into every corner of society and to the ends of the earth. Disciple making is the engine that drives our missional service to those outside the church. We seek to be known where we live for the good that we do in our communities. We love and serve all people, as Jesus did, no strings attached. At the same time, as we do good for others, we also seek to form relational bridges that we prayerfully hope will open doors for teaching people the gospel of the kingdom and the way of salvation.

> *Matthew 28:19–20; Galatians 4:19;*
> *Acts 2:41; Philippians 1:20–21; Colossians 1:27–29;*
> *2 Corinthians 3:3; 1 Thessalonians 2:19–20;*
> *John 13:34–35; 1 John 3:16; 1 Corinthians 13:1–13;*
> *Luke 22:14–23; 1 Corinthians 11:17–24; Acts 20:7.*

8. *Kingdom life.* We believe in the present kingdom reign of God, the power of the Holy Spirit to transform people, and the priority of the local church. God's holiness should lead our churches to reject lifestyles characterized by pride, sexual immorality, homosexuality, easy divorce, idolatry, greed, materialism, gossip, slander, racism, violence, and the like. God's love should lead our churches to emphasize love as the distinguishing sign of

a true disciple. Love for one another should make the church like an extended family—a fellowship of married people, singles, elderly, and children who are all brothers and sisters to one another. The love of the extended church family to one another is vitally important. Love should be expressed in both service to the church and to the surrounding community. It leads to the breaking down of walls (racial, social, political), evangelism, acts of mercy, compassion, forgiveness, and the like. By demonstrating the ways of Jesus, the church reveals God's kingdom reign to the watching world.

> *1 Corinthians 1:2; Galatians 5:19–21;*
> *Ephesians 5:3–7; Colossians 3:5–9;*
> *Matthew 19:3–12; Romans 1:26–32; 14:17–18;*
> *1 Peter 1:15–16; Matthew 25:31–46;*
> *John 13:34–35; Colossians 3:12–13; 1 John 3:16;*
> *1 Corinthians 13:1–13; 2 Corinthians 5:16–21.*

9. *Counter-cultural living.* We believe Jesus' Lordship through Scripture will lead us to be a distinct light in the world. We follow the first and second Great Commandments where love and loyalty to God come first and love for others comes second. So we prioritize the gospel and one's relationship with God, with a strong commitment to love people in their secondary points of need too. The gospel is God's light for us. It teaches us

grace, mercy, and love. It also teaches us God's holiness, justice, and the reality of hell which led to Jesus' sacrifice of atonement for us. God's light is grace and truth, mercy and righteousness, love and holiness. God's light among us should be reflected in distinctive ways like the following:

A. We believe that human life begins at conception and ends upon natural death, and that all human life is priceless in the eyes of God. All humans should be treated as image-bearers of God. For this reason, we stand for the sanctity of life both at its beginning and its end. We oppose elective abortions and euthanasia as immoral and sinful. We understand that there are very rare circumstances that may lead to difficult choices when a mother or child's life is at stake, and we prayerfully surrender and defer to God's wisdom, grace, and mercy in those circumstances.

B. We believe God created marriage as the context for the expression and enjoyment of sexual relations. Jesus defines marriage as a covenant between one man and one woman. We believe that all sexual activity outside the bounds of marriage, including same-sex unions and same-sex marriage, are immoral and must not be condoned by disciples of Jesus.

C. We believe that Jesus invites all races and ethnicities into the kingdom of God. Because humanity has exhibited grave racial injustices throughout history, we believe that everyone, especially disciples, must be proactive in securing justice for people of all races and that racial reconciliation must be a priority for the church.

D. We believe that both men and women were created by God to equally reflect, in gendered ways, the nature and character of God in the world. In marriage, husbands and wives are to submit to one another, yet there are gender specific expressions: husbands model themselves in relationship with their wives after Jesus' sacrificial love for the church, and wives model themselves in relationship with their husbands after the church's willingness to follow Jesus. In the church, men and women serve as partners in the use of their gifts in ministry, while seeking to uphold New Testament norms which teach that the lead teacher/preacher role in the gathered church and the elder/overseer role are for qualified men. The vision of the Bible is an equal partnership of men and women in creation, in marriage, in salvation, in the gifts of the Spirit, and in the ministries of the church but exercised in ways that honor gender as described in the Bible.

E. We believe that we must resist the forces of culture that focus on materialism and greed. The Bible teaches that the love of money is the root of all sorts of evil and that greed is idolatry. Disciples of Jesus should joyfully give liberally and work sacrificially for the poor, the marginalized, and the oppressed.

Romans 12:3–8; Matthew 22:36–40; 1 Corinthians 12:4–7; Ephesians 2:10; 4:11–13; 1 Peter 4:10–11; Matthew 20:24–27; Philippians 1:1; Acts 20:28; 1 Timothy 2:11–15; 3:1–7; Titus 1:5–9; 1 Corinthians 11:2–9; 14:33–36; Ephesians 5:21–33; Colossians 3:18–19; 1 Corinthians 7:32–35.

10. *The end.* We believe that Jesus is coming back to earth in order to bring this age to an end. Jesus will reward the saved and punish the wicked, and finally destroy God's last enemy, death. He will put all things under the Father, so that God may be all in all forever. That is why we have urgency for the Great Commission—to make disciples of all nations. We like to look at the Great Commission as an inherent part of God's original command to "be fruitful and multiply."

We want to be disciples of Jesus who love people and help them to be disciples of Jesus. We are a movement of disciples who make disciples who help renew existing churches and who start new churches that make more disciples. We want to reach as many as possible—until Jesus returns and God restores all creation to himself in the new heaven and new earth.

Matthew 25:31–32; Acts 17:31; Revelation 20:11–15; 2 Thessalonians 1:6–10; Mark 9:43–49; Luke 12:4–7; Acts 4:12; John 14:6; Luke 24:46–48; Matthew 28:19–20; Genesis 12:1–3; Galatians 2:20; 4:19; Luke 6:40; Luke 19:10; Revelation 21:1ff.

NOTES

1. Carol Kuruvilla, "Kansas Governor Sues GOP Leaders for Subverting Order Limiting Church Meetings," *Huffpost*, April 10, 2020, https://www.huffpost.com/entry/kansas-coronavirus-churches-religious-freedom_n_5e90ab2ec5b6d641a6be4d13.

2. See also John 3:36; 5:24; 6:29, 35, 47; 7:38.

3. For more on how faith is more than merely belief or even trust, see Mark Moore's book in the *Real Life Theology* series, *Faithful Faith: Reclaiming Faith from Culture and Tradition* (Renew.org, 2021).

4. "Almost Half of Practicing Christian Millennials Say Evangelism is Wrong," *Barna*, February 5, 2019, https://www.barna.com/research/millennials-oppose-evangelism/.

5. See Acts 2:36; 10:36; 1 Corinthians 8:6; 12:3; 16:22; 2 Corinthians 4:5; Philippians 2:11; Colossians 2:6.

6. Grant R. Osborne, *Romans*, The IVP New Testament Commentary Series (Downers Grove, IL: InterVarsity Press, 2004), 271.

7. Ben Witherington, "Lord," eds. Joel B. Green, I. Howard Marshall, and Scot McKnight, *Dictionary of Jesus and the Gospels* (Downers Grove, IL: InterVarsity Press, 1992), 484.

8. For more on the gospel, see a book in the *Real Life Theology* series by Matthew W. Bates called *The Gospel Precisely: Surprisingly Good News About Jesus Christ the King* (Renew.org, 2021).

9. Thomas Long, *Hebrews*, Interpretation: A Bible Commentary for Teaching and Preaching (Louisville: Westminster John Knox, 1997), 3.

10. For more on how we can hold convictions while cultivating healthy relationships with people we disagree with, see Bobby Harrington and Jason Henderson, *Conviction and Civility: Thinking and Communicating Clearly About What the Bible Teaches* (Renew.org, 2019).

11. John R. W. Stott, *The Message of Romans: God's Good News for the World*, The Bible Speaks Today (Downers Grove, IL: InterVarsity Press, 2001), 359.

Made in the USA
Monee, IL
14 April 2024

56958290R00062